Another & Another

AN ANTHOLOGY FROM THE GRIND DAILY WRITING SERIES

Another & Another

AN ANTHOLOGY FROM THE GRIND DAILY WRITING SERIES

Published by Bull City Press

1217 Odyssey Drive

Durham, NC 27713

http://bullcitypress.com

Another and another: an anthology from the grind daily writing series. /
edited by Matthew Olzmann and Ross White.

   p. cm.

ISBN-13: 978-1-4243-1800-1 (Paperback)

Designed by Lime Tiger

CONTENTS

INTRODUCTION

What you hold in your hands is panic. Or maybe it's pressure. Or a shot in the dark. Blind faith, or determination. Some days it's resignation, others it's a little bit of resilience. It could be a trail of bread crumbs through the forest. That sudden flare of inspiration, or the terror of staring at a page when no words will come. It could be all these things or nothing at all: The Grind Daily Writing Series is a little different for each of its participants.

And it's constantly changing.

The Grind Daily Writing Series started in October 2007, taking a cue from National Poetry Writing Month (or NaPoWriMo). It started with four writers, but grew to include more than 200. It began as only poets, but later incorporated a prose element. It began with writers trying to generate new work, then later expanded with a revision component. What remains the same is that each month, a (constantly shifting) group of writers signs up to create something new each day. And then they do what writers do: they write. Every day. The only catch is that, at the end of the day, they hit "send" and whatever ever they've written goes out to those in their group.

The Grind isn't the first or the only group of writers who have committed to writing each day; in fact, on the next page, we've included the "rules" in case you find that you want to try something similar with an intrepid group of writers. But this particular group has been running without interruption for almost five years now. Some writers participated for seven or eight months in a row, took a month off, then returned again for more. Others entered the fray once and retired.

Most people enter a month of The Grind ready and willing to do the work, and they generally have some ideas or notes that they think will carry them through the month. And occasionally, they do just that. Several chapbook-length products have come from a month of The Grind, and a few folks have finished large swaths of their novels during a month. But for most writers, those ideas and notes fuel about five days' worth of drafts, after which time we're on our own, producing without an agenda. Having to create something new every day quickly wipes out one's reservoir of back-up ideas. Often this leads to sitting down at the writer's table with nothing but the aforementioned feeling of panic. But it also leads to a sense of freedom and bouts of intense experimentation. It leads to self-imposed formal challenges. It leads to topics one wouldn't have dared tackle if there had been more time to think things over.

What developed wasn't simply a group of people writing each day, but a community that embraced a messy, chaotic process. A community of eager readers. As much as The Grind is about producing new work, it's also about watching other writers reach deep, watching other writers push through the dry spell or conjure from sparse materials. The Grind gives its participants the opportunity not only to see the work but to see how it is created, to see it in its nascent stages.

What we tried to do, in putting this collection together, is capture some of that wildness. Each of these poems was initially drafted while the author was participating in The Grind, though what you read here has been revised and polished many times since. This is not a "best-of" anthology, nor does it include every writer who has attempted the endeavor; it's a snap shot, a slide show, a sampling of the first two years of The Grind Daily Writing Series.

—Matthew Olzmann & Ross White
Co-Coordinators, The Grind Daily Writing Series

THE RULES

Basically, there are only two rules to The Grind Daily Writing Series:

• Write one new, completed draft each day. Poets must finish a draft of a poem, prose writers must finish something, be it a page or paragraph, a scene or character sketch. The Grind is about completing new work. So finish it.

• Drafts sent by other writers should never be shared. Please, no matter how much you loved a draft, respect that the author may not view this as finished work and may not want anyone else on earth to see it. For some people, just sharing with this group is harrowing enough. And if you're copying non-Grinders on your e-mails, please let your Grind-mates know, so they don't accidentally hit "Reply-All" and send to people who aren't participating.

There's some other miscellaneous stuff you should know:

• If you're new to The Grind, or you didn't participate last month, you have to write one draft every day. No skipping a day and making it up later. If you participated last month, you can elect to take a day off no more than once per week—if you must (yawn)—for a total of 26 drafts in 30 days.

• There are no restrictions on form and no minimum line length. A one-line poem will suffice just as nicely as a 28-page masterpiece.

• Drafts must be sent to all participants by midnight. As we've regularly spread ourselves across the entire country, the term "midnight" refers to your own time zone. If you travel, obey the time zone you're going to be in when you go to bed.

• Some days will be rotten, and so will some drafts; no excuses. Write something—anything—every day or suffer the mockery, derision, and eternal scorn of the other writers.

• Feedback is not part of the equation—if we get all self-congratulatory for good first drafts, the silence surrounding the bad stuff will start to sting. So, if you really love a draft, feel free to say something, but don't feel like you need to (or should) comment on poems daily. We're not sending to each other to congratulate, but to feel (and be) accountable to the process and try something we might not have otherwise tried.

• Participation in The Grind is by invitation only—you must be invited by someone who completed the last month to which they committed. If you want to bring others into this community, you'll have to complete the month.

Another & Another

AN ANTHOLOGY FROM THE GRIND DAILY WRITING SERIES

THINKING OF HIS JAYWALKING TICKET
WHILE BOARDING A PLANE AT SFO

Years ago, he refused to pay it. He said
city officials painted a crosswalk
straight from police department
to donut shop. His refusal

won't land him in Gitmo.
He's not in the slammer.
And this is not the Texan town where
your sister's called *another dirty Mexican*

waiting in the ER all night with cold
coffee and a feverish child. Not *spray-of-glass
at-the-back-of-your-sundress*
Ohio where you once

fed stale bread to ducks.
He's seated at your side,
elbow to elbow, prepared
to grow slack-jawed over books.

Years ago, he'd found no
safe way to walk from that bus stop,
no path for the workers
waiting to dash through traffic gaps,

no end to his disbelief when the officer
issued a ticket for crossing four lanes.

Years ago, and still
you feel fear's pin-prick

when you hear the words
alien, raid. Detained. Deported.
The plane seats fill and fill
while, in your mind, his seat

empties and empties—as your mouth empties
and your lungs empty each time you hear
we need to ask a few questions.
No one has approached

your aisle, for now. You're safe
to begin your own
cross-examination:
Which swallowed Arabic vowel

will trap him this time?
Which sandpaper *Anwar?*
Which fish-bone *Khalid?*
You'd like to tease and say,

*Mothers, do not name
your sons Mohammed.* But
you do not joke anymore.
You don't joke about anything.

Dilruba Ahmed

DEAR MASOOM

We are happy to hear
you have electric in your home,
that the pipes by each window
keep you warm. What a kind
government to provide
milk, butter, and cheese.
Arey, if only ours would do the same—
but it can't keep the trash
off the capital's streets.
We hope you and Shilpa are well.
The little ones, send them
our love. Please come home soon.
Boro Bhai would like
to see you before he dies.

The blankets you mailed
are quite fine—Maya and I share
one, as I gave mine
to Boro Bhai. He coughs and rasps
all night despite the ginger tea.
I can hardly sleep
for the noise. Boro Bhai is getting older,
you know, so the monsoons make him
wheeze, the dust makes him wheeze,
changes in weather make him wheeze.
I hear him now as I sit
wrapped in the one blanket
Maya and I share.

Brother, we are well
in most regards. We are keeping
warm in the sweaters you mailed
last year, the dry season upon us
already. At night the chill could break
your bones. Just last week
the *shim* vine's beans grew as shiny
as eggplant, but now a jinn
rises in the fields.

EVENING IN MENDOCINO

You're blanketed in the
smell of sea kelp, plant
that moves like animal.

Who wouldn't believe
in mermaids? The ocean
is lonely. Forget

long walks at sunset, etc.
Something here is
ripe. Something grown

from salt. It could wrap
you in strands
so soft you would gladly

give in. Relinquish
your name, your story,
your life. Then sink

to the root of it, anchor
yourself to one water-
darkened rock. Surrender

to sound. Let sunlight
become a memory,
barely recognized or felt.

DREAM: THE DISAPPEARED LOVER

The slope of her back.
Petite teacups
against the hurled aggressions of the day.
After dinner, she unscrews
her tin shoulder and pours out her
cracked-bone paraffin. It pleases
me to have her disjointed. Makes
me feel safe to have her
grounded.
I oil her and watch
as she whirrs. Sesame, pork
fat. We grow our meal, her hand
down my throat, my teeth up
her thigh.
The wet ground holds us in,
bakes us a familiar
taste.
We sit inside,
licking the lips off our beloved.

CHINESE WORKERS AT USDA LAB, 1904

the fathers don't remember
        being born

moths in the vegetable garden   shotguns piercing white

sheets wide-brimmed

hat with eyes steel and pulley

I wonder if the last father dying among chickens and bombed-out
cars remembers

            the look of one who sees over
                rather than upon   an object cradled and weighed
        loved into minerals

            the man whose name drowned
    in the photograph   all I have
    his upper body
                        a grasping hand
    lift beyond this America
                        a belly tree full
    of dust my father selling
            vegetables grown from bone

AMERICAN SYNTAX

The teacher straightbacked,
faced me off, her eyes.
My face in the cleave of
her shoulder, my bones
sitting high my cheek.
The word proper
arrives in the hall. The order
of things, rolling
neat into pine drawers, dead-
clean. Squeezed juice of greedy
sponge.
Her teeth not match.
One chipped. The corner lifted,
peeking a window, furtive.
The other, pearl, round
and perfect, looming above my
arched head. About to bite.

Ching-In Chen

THE SENTENCE LOVERS

after Larissa Lai

The sentence lovers are complete and independent in and of themselves.
The sentence lovers don't need you.
The sentence lovers aren't dependent on others who withhold the missing clauses from the story.
The sentence lovers do not follow. They don't want to be hanging off a cliff.
The sentence lovers desire.
Sometimes they write of rebellion only to wake up at the point of departure from a dream.

Then insert comma.

The sentence lovers forget the face of the fragment. They think this is war.
The sentence lovers feel good about their wholeness. Round bodies filled with the correct vocabulary.

The standard syntax.

The sentence lovers do not deviate. Take responsibility for your verb.
For the sea makes no sense without
you putting yourself back into your sentence.

NIGHTS

In her silvery room sleeps
the young Miss Egmont,
her profile as on an ancient coin,
her body glowing
like the great barrier reef;

austere, remote, she floats in darkness.
Out at sea the oil derrick
burns through the night
scribbling on the water
an orange alphabet.

It is like this every night here:
you are the younger Miss Egmont,
you are the barrier reef,
you are the sirocco in the palms,
you the pillar of fire shooting out
your distress flares into the vacant night—
the ones I can see for miles,
the ones I no longer answer.

WE BURIED TIME IN YOUR BACKYARD

I don't remember a thing we placed in it,
but after all, the shined blue Folger's canister
swaddled in duct tape was concession

to the hard weight of matter outliving memory.
I remember this: We believed that one day

we would find our way back to that coffee can
planted in your driveway. We counted paces
from your back door, painted cardboard maps,

tacked them to trees, snugged one rolled-up sheaf
in the crook of the oak overhanging the river—

with no thought to the elements, no understanding
of how quickly the world will whittle away
what no longer lives. Time, a teacher would say

years after you were gone, *is the passing of reality
as defined by repetitive events,* but it was not

something I could make sense of with either a trowel
at ten or a calculator at twenty. You moved out west
and we wrote until we did not. No one I know

knows exactly where you are. Somewhere in Arizona
you tend the sick. You were my blood sister the night

we spied on your mother and stepfather
through their half-closed bedroom door.
It's not a sin, you whispered, and I had not

until that moment considered that it, or anything,
might be. I have been back to your driveway, Ann.

It is sinuous and overgrown, a path to nowhere
since your trailer was towed away. I looked
under each young tree, each sprig of grass,

as though that coffee canister were a seed
from which something should have grown up.

MINOR GHOST HOTEL

pardon that clicking   the ghost
> of some prick haunts these halls

the paintings on the walls
> seem to be rising like dough

pardon the busts and the torsos
> and the feet which sometimes assemble

and shamble around as one body

I want to prevent
> this disaster of unity

for once I want to move
> faster than adagio

I fear the shape these words
> could make if they were alive

so I cripple them with impossibility

THICKET

Having listened to *This American Life*
and finding I have not lived an American life,
I wander into the thicket looking
for something to eat. The thicket this time of night
is forbidden, so only those in a mind like mine
come here—it's like a singles bar just for melancholics,
moon-people and comics.
In the thicket there are berries I know
and then there are otherberries.
Outside the thicket my name is Travis Smith
but here they call me Aubergine, that is
to say "Eggplant," and I'm fine with that, that is beautiful:
The moon is a vacuum tube
that will zip down on us, soon.

FABLE #7

You were the calligrapher
whose job it was to copy

texts precisely, gracefully,
each letter distinct, a blade of grass.

I was a reed
growing on a riverbank. You came

absent-mindedly with a knife and
cut me into a shape you could use.

FABLE #6

You were sleep, and
I was summer rain.

You were the notebook
lying open on the red couch
so that one of your pages
lifted, fell, lifted in a
current of air, and
I was gravity,
just barely keeping you there.

You were a painting
leaning against an empty fireplace, and
I was the threat—slight,
but present all the same—of fire.

You were shadows
cast by a ceiling fan that
turned just fast enough to
move the air.
I was a mirror
on the wall over the fireplace;
you turned in me too.

You weren't the white wallpaper.
You weren't the fleur-de-lis.
You weren't the growl of empty stomachs.

I was not the television.

You were sleep, and
I was the darkness
in which you came running.

Rosalynde Vas Dias

ARGUMENT

Love is the dragon
gorging on his own spilled

entrails—in support of this assertion
I present this photo: a pond

of paramecium begetting
more paramecium among drowned

tires. To support the photo,
this document detailing

the emergency procedure
at the clown college. Don't

laugh. Clowns too need a place
to learn and that institution

requires policies. To support
the emergency procedure:

this exhibit—a baggie
of air exhaled

from the lungs of a man stricken,
miraculously recovered,

and stricken, miraculously, once
more. To support the baggie—

this unlit match expressing the potential
to consume the dead man's breath.

To support the match this final evidence:
Our last. Bitter and bright and earnest

as we carried the compost
to the garden. And the embrace.

And your leave-taking and me inside,
locking the door.

ALL ACTUALLY

Inevitable that clouds
veil the sky
the night I determine
to navigate by celestial
bodies. I steer by the one star available—
really an olive-colored
Scout flashlight.

Or is it the 'Star'
Card (#17) meaning,
in part, "There is a burning nugget
of phosphorous
right under your tongue.
Open your mouth to see the way"?

After blundering about in the light
of this uncertain object(s), I find
it is almost fall. I am in a well-tended
lot of sunflowers—
so many suns! All actually
stars! Or is it
the opposite?

Matthew Olzmann

TORQUE

We know gears are supposed to turn,
but we forget their teeth, that to pull
they must bite into another.

Last month, the workers at the axle factory
went on strike. Without the axle,
there is no car. Without the carloads

of workers at noon, the sandwich shop
down the block shuts its doors,
kills its lights. Behind the sandwich shop,

a dumpster filled with bees.
My wife is allergic to the stinger.
Lodged in human skin, the barb is lost

to the bee, and the bee must die.
And if enough of them fail again
to find the hive, that dies as well.

SIR ISAAC NEWTON'S FIRST LAW OF MOTION

Objects in motion will remain in motion unless
acted upon by an outside force. Objects
at rest will remain at rest unless acted upon
by an outside force. Matthew Olzmann
is an object at rest, and will remain at rest,
reclining on the couch while drinking Guinness
and watching football. Or, he is an object at rest,
and will remain at rest, sprawled over the couch
while drinking Guinness and watching hockey.
Or, he could be merely napping on the couch,
having already finished a Guinness,
and though the TV is on, he's not watching,
because it's three in the afternoon and there's nothing
to watch. Where does Matthew Olzmann go
when he shuts his lovely eyes and dreams
his lovely dreams about drinking Guinness
while hunting saber-toothed tigers? Obviously,
he goes nowhere. Let me say this again. The man
is an object at rest, a legendary object at rest,
and will remain at rest unless acted upon
by his wife, who comes home shortly
and will remind him to take out the garbage
or go to the grocery store. Matthew Olzmann
would have performed these duties by now,
but it's hard to rise from this couch,
impossible actually, if one believes in physics.
Matthew Olzmann believes in physics.
Let no one say he did not believe.

Matthew Olzmann

ENGINE IN THE SHAPE OF A TINY METAL DOG

In one of Diego Rivera's murals, Henry Ford
lectures a group of auto workers.
Between them, an engine. From the engine,
the gear shaft grows tail-like, two disks
appear as eyes, four legs sprout from the base.
The docent points to that dog and explains:
in pre-Columbian graves ceramic dogs
were buried to guide the spirit from one world
to the other. So too, we're told,
the engine guides us from one era to another.
Something felt off with the analogy—
when a man sits behind a wheel, he expects
to reach his destination alive. Still, I wondered
what I might be buried with when I make my exit.
What hound sleeps outside my door,
ready to lead me from a city of empty warehouses
to a clearing of river birch and moonlight?
Last week, I attended a funeral far from home.
My fear, a coyote's call in the distance.
My hesitation, the slowing of four black tires, the rasp
of gravel underneath. Exhausted from driving
across three states, I didn't know what to say
when an usher at the church told me
I needed to find God—as if God was a location,
an X on a map. But as I looked at the usher,
then the faces of the bereaved, in the middle
of a city whose roads made little sense,

there might have been an animal made of iron
on the grounds, but I couldn't summon the strength
to track it down or language to make it heel.

RITUAL

The church doesn't love
the matador.
Ole ole ole ole ole ole ole ole ole ole ole ole ole!

NIGHT

Little bull,
dancing at the well's
mouth.
Matador riding
the black bottom.

MATADOR

Beauty that is not shaped is heart-buckled
Beauty lives across the divide from the other-shaped beauty
I have lived on the other side of beauty
I have lived this side of beauty
Beauty the scale we measure loss against
Beauty the fence
Beauty the fence we climb
Beauty the hole we step through
Make a hole-shaped place for beauty
Each hour a sacrifice to beauty
Beauty sacrifices itself

LOVE

A matador can't be
too careful.
A thing beating,
on its knees.

SEX

She's looking at me
like I have cake
in my hair.

RIVER WALK

If I drink enough   Knob Creek,
I might fistfight   for Frank O'Hara
as a shark-eyed   poet shouts:
He wrote quotidian   rambles on napkins.
If suddenly,   sanctimoniously,
I could exorcise   his exclamations,
bring Frank's   body back
from frozen sleep   off Fire Island,
might he squeeze   my square shoulders
at said party where   I'm slurring speech?

Just past   the pig farm,
I come   hung over
as the bent   bamboos in the wood
where finally   I wrestle off
winter's striped   wool scarf
to amble   along the Swannanoa.
Rapids are at   restorative reach
as we watch   as wild vines
thick as thighs   tying themselves
to tulip poplars   persist, insist,
supersede.   Now she's
rolling downhill   through ditch rose
as shapes of ice   slide, then slip,
sheer silhouettes,   out of sight.

If we were   to stay within
tender rings   of fallen timber,

what horizon   would hold
    our breath   without breaking?

FROM: MRS. MARIA BEJES
SUBJECT: CHARITY FOR HUMANITY

She comes to me as a burning vision, out of the dark
unexpected, her words on the page honey to my eyes.

Names me beloved, chooses me to scatter her wealth
like so many breadcrumbs across the yard of the world.

Ten million three hundred thousand dollars is not
birdseed. It is a fruitful transaction, the good work

Of the Lord, and one hell of a shaft to her shiftless
relatives. No matter. Mrs. Maria Bejes has packed

Her do-good dough into Diplomatic Luggage, waiting
to verify when the charmingly named truckbox is claimed.

Out of so many, to be called. Mrs. Maria Bejes, light
of my inbox, I say yes. Yes to your charity. Yes to faith.

Yes to proper use of the imperative *nota bene*. But
Mrs. Maria Bejes, you had me at "dear beloved."

"DOES IT FEEL LIKE A TOOTHACHE IN YOUR LEG OR THIGH?"

Rolled-up newspaper with just this
headline showing, your empathy
unnerves a morning walk. Will you
hold my hand as the dentist picks
and mirrors the offending limb?
I've grown six wisdom teeth against
all odds—number seven could incubate
anywhere. Freud, too, would nod
his head, expecting vaginal teeth
that go vagrant, feral, their dental
march downward a migration
of desire over time. I've chewed
up love and spit it out, but now
you expose me to myself, headline.
The pain that beats in my leg
(or thigh) could be a heart hard
as molars, could be mine.

STUTTER STUTTER

I do this for the prospect of edification.
I learn by numbers.

I do this louder than prayer –
contemptuous of my enemies,
I shriek like the soul of a mute.

Leave warbling to songbirds.
Leave chirping to babies,
things that flit above gutters.

Because I am a salesman,
I do this as guarantee –
door-to-door, I proselytize.

I do, darling, I do this
to be certain of your love,
to breathe, to heat your January palms.

I rid words from my body,
where they have swarmed my lungs,
have come to take up space.

I do this as an act of blistering.
I grind my teeth to cosmic dust.

Words echo in my lusty chamber.

Like a hummingbird, frenetic am I.
Impatient. Least of all, free.

I must make hollow this world.
I must fill it.

SCHADENFREUDE

I have to write this poem for you,
the girl apparently sober

enough to ride the late night van in circles
one Saturday of our freshman year,

orbiting the quad like an overlord,
a common buzzard hacking

at the freeze of her own life
with throaty laugh, speckled cackle –

the van's wheels spinning free of snow
to finally expose the truth:

Girls like me get drunk.

We drown every cell in drink
in mutual gratification, disgust,

the sinking feeling in our gut
anchoring us to this earth if for a moment.

We, bleak with drink, drunk on bleakness,
don't blink, don't flinch through it.

We animal, our souls raw hide,
leave a rocky trace of blood,

noticing it only miles later,
our clean claws, our wretched underbellies.

We, stupid drunk, come upon ourselves
alone in the night and remember:

We don't even like the taste.

In your article for the school paper, you quoted me:
Nobody at this school cares about another.

Tell me that I was wrong.

How you walked right into that one. How you sat shotgun
right into that one, over and over. Face it,

you need a drunk girl like me
more than I need a drink.

Your life, a series of contingencies.
Your face, like your writing: forgettable.

A LITTLE DICKENS

For JB

I want to stop writing about birds,
and I believe this is the first step.

Yesterday I awoke in the sterling silver light
on a bed of traffic violation confetti

in a world where *illiteracy* meant *drunk*
with negative capability

and I didn't feel pushed around by the world,
hurtled into indecision, soot spread

across the apples of my cheeks
like a Victorian caricature. I was poor

and obscure, and not in a charming
or hopeful way. I was a graduate student

writing about birds, and I was ugly and alone
in my knowledge that it's much easier to torture

schoolchildren if one gets paid by the word.
How now a masochist like me loved *David Copperfield*—

the oscillation of plot, the manhandling of the reader—
it's all very offensive in taste like porridge

like tattered pant hems, like thousand-page books,
and please, sir, may I have another and another.

TESTAMENT

If only I believed the rain were real,
I would not feel so wet.

But this world does not lend itself
to belief. Consider the clouds,
that they are supposedly water, and yet
lighter than air.

This is absolutely ridiculous.
Any child will tell you so.

But, if you require proof, find two
five-gallon buckets.
Fill one with water,
and the other with atmosphere,
and see which one gives
your little sister a hernia.

You may consider this experiment
mean-spirited, but consider this,

Dear Reader:
I do not believe you will try it.

Dearest Reader, I do not believe in you.

Henry Kearney, IV

SOME SIMPLE TRUTHS

Moving to Italy is not the same as dying,
though one can be forgiven for making this mistake.
The fact seems obvious, yet many people every day
get caught up in this very confusion; oblivion being so often sought,
yet so elusive by nature. If one is of such a mind,
there are other, less financially stressing activities (such as
fly-fishing, or fencing, or skateboarding) in which one can
"lose oneself" or "forget oneself" as one's desires bend.
However, none of these (bowling? learning piano? fashioning
countless variations of Saint Brigid's cross?) seem
satisfactory for those truly committed to oblivion.
There is nothing, in fact, that seems satisfactory
except, perhaps, and when performed properly, the act
of love-making. This, however, requires at least one
other person, and is rarely done properly (which,
as we have already decided, is a prerequisite for the inclusion
of the act in our current discussion). Yet, I do believe it is proper
to include it. Yes, I am certain it is proper to speak now
of love-making as a means of moving towards oblivion,
for it is astounding what this particular oblivion may create.
If you are fortunate enough to find a like-minded partner,
and still more fortunate that one morning or evening or noon or midnight
the two of you combine forces and perform the act properly
(this will take practice, which I strongly encourage),
beware in the immediate aftermath any and all mirrors.
You will not recognize what you find there.

YOUNG TOURISTS

In the afternoon the bricks ringing
in sunlight across the square.
All is glare, summer-dull.
Two people walking towards a home
temporary in nature. Temporal all.
There is no moral. Sharing a language
(not theirs) and little else, save a sense of being
vaguely lost but comfortable,
almost arm in arm they stumble,
fumbling with unfamiliar prepositions,
another bottle of wine, muted
propositions. Each unsure of owning intent.
"It is lovely, is it no?"
"No, it is."

SUI CAEDERE (DISAMBIGUATION)

Between the backside
of Mexico and the military

base half a stitch to LA,
a railroad track loiters

like a Santa Ana due.
Two fat avocados cook

on a kitchen counter.
Laundered diapers hang

against a thick sky. Everyone still
asleep. September still

listless with the blot
of summer. Beside the track

a late model silver sedan, six months
paid for, windows sealed.

Coffee and bagel still
waiting. A guy in khakis and tie asleep

at the wheel. You're sure
he'll wake up. You're sure

he's asleep. There's a tsunami
in Sumatra, a shooting

in Vegas, a baby born without eyes
up the coast. Someone orders

a margarita, salt like grit
on the rim. Someone orders another.

Everyone else drinks beer. It goes down
like water, but here

the gully is dry, sun austere,
wind blue, and a shadow

like a man in a box dumped
beside trestle and creek.

Even at this hour, it looks
like a safe place to sleep.

Tamiko Beyer

BOUNDARY LINE

St. Louis

Mississippi heaves; Lewis and Clark drown.
The river eddies its tongue across their bronze chests,
licks Clark's cleft chin, swallows the tip of an elbow.
I bike under the gateway's hot gleam.

East, the water drags reflected sky: a surprised blue
between spindly, spit-off trees. Graveyard to the west –
row after lozenged row of hoods popped open,
gapings where engines once hummed.
North, against the river a water treatment plant
fumes and a white plaque marks

where nine people once set across the midnight river
to cross a border, sail that invisible line
riding the surface: Missouri slave, Illinois free.
But neither sheriff nor Henry Shaw were men
to lose their goods so easy. They waited
on the other shore, the May night so close
against their faces they might have drowned.
Though no one went under, pistols went off,
shackles on, and bodies dragged back. Whippings
to blood and a mother sold downriver.

all this I carry and all this I ferry and my banks are mud and my banks
are mud and I shine only what the sky gives me your children will come

to my banks of mud and your name not on my tongue and your name not

on their tongues I swallow the stars and I eat your tears and I have all these

years carried this body this body this bank loosened this mud I eat and

I will never and you will never some future swallow and at the end of all this

a gulf and at the end of all this a body so warm I lose myself

in tributary your name as salt this salt a gull a gully a gull a gully

WHAT MELTS YOUR ICE TEETH, WHAT SHATTERS

My family cannot say
why you and I stay, here

where night lasts
a whole season.

Their autumn blazes
exhaust to sodden mess,

but here winter settles
quick, effortless. Like bears

we layer our bones:
muscle, fat, skin.

Wool and down,
we fasten scarves

across our vulnerable mouths.
Isn't this what it means to be human?

Under the moon's bastard light
I'm trying to hear

you between the roars
of your lovely demons.

Depression is an imprint
on the snow,

rabbit track or moose –
see, see how I can mimic,

clown? See the water
on our lashes freeze

to pure prism? Love,
let me save us here

where wind marks
our bodies edges –

what exhilaration,
so close to frozen.

No icicle glint,
only snow's blank,

sculpted body and
whatever we utter

the north air takes
from us.

Come in from the elements,
whittled, sheared –

our bodies caught in the briefest light.

Tamiko Beyer

sweet branch stitched to bitter tree

After many sleight-of-hand days the sun squares itself on the white walls. *Tart* is what your tongue says against the slice you lay across it. *Sweet* say your molars. What kind of graft makes an apple worth eating?

our body's report –
a seed myth, stem tale, a lie
starred in every core

WADE

1.
because no disaster is perfect
there are mistakes made
made in every single disaster
because

in the diffuse
light
after
the rain
dawn becomes
a hesitant
mirror
because

                    we
in an attic
watch
the slow rise
water thick
inside and out
become a drenched
hug a mouth
that envelopes
because

no air

I received conflicting information
I received information
approximately
the levees had broken
I received
conflicting information
later the levees
information
only topped
because

2.
after
the neighbor
and his raft
we wade

we spend
the next night
in an abandoned
bus

3.
Dear responsibility,
are you lonely?

4.
pink plastic curler
safety pin toothbrush
nested in sweating mud

what
longs for hair
for teeth for tether

we are only bodies

we exhaust in moments

we turn in increments
of light's
slow rise

Note: italicized lines taken from testimony by Michael Brown, former director of Federal Emergency Management Agency (FEMA) during 2005 Congressional hearings.

METROPOLIS

Stress this: the lit end
of anything will burn you.
Stress this: running will never
save you. The day after
Christmas a body was given
back to the dirt, & that's just
a slick way of saying
Malik's first son caved,
fell to the pressure, to the indent
the barrel made against
his temple. Stress this:
we never gave a fuck,
not about Malik or how
the bullet didn't split
the air, but split the edged up,
precise hairs on caesar. &
we're all Brutus, saving a man
years of fearing death.

FOR THE CITY THAT NEARLY BROKE ME

I tell my son that it's all counter
intuitive, the art of breathing
bullets, it's all about walking down
the street and staring the tough guy
on the corner in the eye, it's all
remembering that a thug
is a misnomer. I tell him to think
about the homeless man dying
a green light at a time as cars
zoom past. That's what living
in this city is, mastering the timing
of failure. Wouldn't it be a good thing if
the art of not breaking the ground with
your body wasn't as important as
the sum of a missed bus and darkness?
I tell my son this city teaches
a man how to be naked with all his
clothes on, how to believe a prison
is nothing more than a long way home.

Reginald Dwayne Betts

THE FIRST NIGHT AHMAD CAME HOME

He dreams of farina & fried eggs,
& he hungers for the secret
of a sentence that doesn't end,
of how to heft his weight
into a job interview & speak
as if the prison walls themselves
aren't filling his lungs with whispers
& wanting—he dreamed all this,
he dreamed a room, a little piece
of a world he owns where there's
a wild echo in the way he stretches
his arms in the middle of this first night,
complaining to himself about the softness
of a mattress he doesn't deserve, &
that he can't make more than a memory
of the rugged thin heap that held up
his body at night when his mind refused

WHAT WE DIDN'T KNOW BEFORE MARVIN GAYE DIED

One day a knife would scrape the ridges off
his voice and leave his lowest note half-coughed.

And I'd make love to a woman listening to mercy
mercy me as if my sweating body wasn't kerosene,

wasn't another way to beg my way into forgiveness
or turn making love into a way to finesse

a song from a body shackled to the blues.
Each day was always a Monday running into

Friday in my head, always the devil's shaking
dice rattling in my cupped palms. Marvin would sing

to the wildness that creased my bones into a threat
and broke my spirit to pay this wild woman's debt.

AT THE END OF LIFE, A SECRET

Everything measured. A man twists
a tuft of your hair out for no reason
other than you are naked before him
and he is bored. Moments ago he was weighing
your gallbladder, and then he was staring
at the empty space where your lungs were.
Even dead, we still say you are an organ donor,
as if some things other than taxes outlast
death. Your feet are regular feet. Two of them,
and there is no mark to suggest you were
an expert mathematician, that you were
the first runner up in debate championships '56,
Tapioca, Ill. From the time your dead
body was carted before him, to the time your
dead body is being sent to the coffin,
every pound is accounted for, except 22 grams.
The man is a praying man & has figured
what it means. He says this is the soul
that has left, finally, after the breath has gone.
The soul: less than 4,000 dollars worth of crack
—22 grams—is all that moves you through this world.

METROPOLIS

There is always blood,
& there is always what
we don't do about it:
the crayons broken in
hallways crowded with piss,
the last swig of a bottle
that's known too many hands.
Malik's head slumped
in his brother's lap.
I once saw a man drinking
beer on a stoop with his son,
passing their kept secrets
through the brown liquid
they sipped. Malik
makes me think
about beer splashing against
concrete, & the stories
that knives make disappear.
We only tell parts of stories.
We want to need a way
to believe in grief, to handle
our lives with the audacity of riding
the Metro bus for seven stops
to get to a school on the other side
of the city. That audacity.

Nicelle Davis

ENOUGH TIME

There is a cold river being pulled through the eye of a needle. There are hands marked by fire from putting a baby out—white nightgown up with a match—

these fingers pinch and pull the silver thread down my back. She is my grandmother. I am seven. She is making me a black velvet dress for Christmas, but

hasn't time for a zipper. She is married to a man who at twelve tosses his five siblings from a second story window before dragging his father's kerosene-

doused body from their burning house. Flesh separating from bone—paper man. Rasp of breath. Effort: that final unsaid word. His father will melt in

his arms. Stick to his skin. He will drop bombs in Vietnam. She will sell vacuums door to door with two girls, twins, a baby trailing behind her. Her

children: curious matches. My mother will have red half moons burned into her belly with a cigarette lighter. Her sister, at fifty, won't know why. They

will leave their mother in a dentist's waiting room. They will be hours late in picking her up. A cup of blood in her mouth. She will say nothing when they

fetch her. Her husband will use her false teeth as a puppet. Chase after his wife
with her own bite. I want to love her gums, but she refuses to undress her

mouth in front of me. At Christmas dinner, when the conversation is years away from me—I arch my back to break the dress seam—for the sound of tearing open—for the attention of coming apart. I think it will be funny. This is the only time I will ever see my grandmother cry. Later she will tell me stories

of the Great Depression—how she spent a penny to see a flushing toilet. She will have me piss in a pot to understand. She will promise to bare a smile when I turn

sixteen. She will look at her hands and say, *we do what we can—even when it isn't enough. You understand?* I will nod yes and mean no. She will die when I am

thirteen. I'll never feel like I loved her enough. I'll love her more than any.

IT WAS EASIER TO MANAGE

I started kindergarten that fall you went off to Guyana.
Granny cut off my dreadlocks. She knew how to press

and curl, ponytail and cornrow but palm-roll
locks till the roots stiffen with beeswax,

glisten like licorice, she didn't know.
For that matter, no one in the Projects knew

what to do with hair left natural, left
unparted and wild—they were afraid to touch

unmothered parts of themselves. Each snip
made each one alive and each one dead.

And if you said goodbye, it was an honest whisper,
short and fine in your throat.

She cut my hair like a boy
who hadn't been to the barber for a month,

and I sat at the cafeteria table alone for weeks.
They couldn't make sense of me, my classmates

with their gender-proper hairstyles, I didn't
want anything to do with franks and beans;

pucks of grilled meat. I waited at lunchtime
for peanut butter and jelly and was hesitant to eat

bread that wasn't the color of you. It was hard
not hearing your voice each morning,

throughout the day; and unwilling to correct them
when they said my name wrong, I gave into

the Sizzlean, the fried chicken crunched
between my teeth, I could've bitten both of your hands

for leaving me here; each finger for the gunshots that rang
the night, the footsteps running on the roof, the gravel mashed

deeper and deeper into my sleep, flocks of butterflies
broke my skin and I was shatter where I stood,

a whole constellation of wondering if I threw
myself to the sky, coated it with furious wishes

you'd see I missed you, that the barter was unfair,
that you mistook me for sheep.

SIMONE COUSTEAU ON THE OCEAN FLOOR

Straight down through the sharks,
her only option to fall.

Aqua-lung half-full, she descends—
to ascend would mean death:

bobbing, bait on the surface
above black eyes. Never

this many, not even with steak
from the Calypso's crow's nest.

Twenty Great Whites. She counts
again. Their skin, which no one

realizes, rough, not meant
for petting. She wishes she had

worn her emerald earrings,
if this is the moment, if this is it.

Jacques, the children content
that it was at sea. She thinks of

going ahead, pricking finger with hair pin.
Quick. They can smell a drop

three miles away. She's drawn
these fish before, in water the color

of drowning. Once in the cage,
she stuck a hand through wet

bars to feel a fin, massive, cold.
In a minute, she'll be holding her breath.

Laurie Saurborn Young

BRIAR PATCH

Let's consider the unsculpted side of the page,
or ways boiling water will steal a peach's skin.
Think on how attic stairs fold flat angles
into the ceiling, or guess why a woman turned away
was always a favorite pose. I can provide
only two examples of radial symmetry—
crown-of-thorns or *brittle star*. Reasons
I keep a dog around involve my love
of stray hair and missing the nail's quick.
Take that peach skin again, we have a pelt,
thin no fruit just fuzzy deflation fully
absolved of its sugar. Tonight I read the letters,
learning over the myriad ways my name
and *darling* might be misspelled. Funny how they
all rhyme with fly paper, with creosote, with tar.

THE MAKING OF HISTORY

Writing about dogs becomes boring
when it continually features the same dog.
True as well for lovers and methods
of setting a fire. The wind today crashes,

sends pine needles up in sprays. Look—
now as above, the same applies
to the pastoral. How thick will meadows
become, how far away can a habited

voice turn? How many times can one
word be underlined? Any answer
is only a guess, a blind stab at knowing
the best way to set a table. Eras existed

without chairs or pockets, and yet
we survived, we eventually evolved
to the middle land of between-standing-
and-squatting; of jangling-loose-change

against thin cotton and our skin. Days
are spent tracing text in this backward
fashion, examining lines of a broken
company, lost somewhere on the heath

where little claws through and fires burn
short. The dog is only asleep. The weather

just happens to be fervent. Forks best
on the left, spoons suited to the right.

David Ruekberg

CHRISTMAS EVE

The taste of Jesus
when I was five

was plastic and white
with a little gold paint.

The booklet of Beatitudes
so crinkled and waxy,

sky blue and warm peach
and creamy.

The music of Jesus
was sweet and sad.

The nails in his palms
like roses.

How I wished
I could join him

up there, so sweetly
suffering.

The rooms of my house
so square and solid.

The blue of the walls
dim in the corners.

David Ruekberg

LOOKING OUT

Look how this morning
the light returns to our back yard
and fields behind it.

Now the night is a memory
and in place of the absence
which gives it form
is a color we call black.

And look how on the lawn
the white snow has melted,
revealing circles of green
like islands, some,

or little planets scattered
and forming, in my mind,
a kind of constellation,

and others massed, whole galaxies,
or, as some call them,
patches, as if the ground
were quilted with them.

And how, under its sheet of snow
the yard merges with the sleeping
field and its yellow stubble.
Or dun, or brown, or ochre.

And how the field becomes a hill,
climbs, becomes trees which
reach up with grey and purple
fingers. Or magenta, or sumac.

Or black, against a sky
where, after three days of rain
and grey, the white clouds part,

touched with a little rose
from the morning sun,
and behind those, blue,

finally, after three days,
and behind that, something
large that we compare,
finally, to night.

Shann Palmer

DESIRE

With every revolution
history rewrites itself.

I would know your body
in my sleep, the soft curve
against the pillow, my hand

reaching, then letting go.

Ross White

MODERN PROBLEMS

The problem with modern fiction is flora: it's quite literary
to pepper the ground with cedar, jasmine, jacaranda, chokecherry,
all willy-nilly without respect to climate. The problem with now
is that the past is a pickaxe, an archaeologist with a furrowed brow
chiseling around the edges of what was meant to remain a secret.
The problem with beaches is erosion; made of granite,
they would not be sloughing off into the ocean, which, incidentally,
is warming, and that is the problem with it, though I could name two or three.
The problem with tuna salad is mayonnaise. The problem with art
is proving its problematic value. The problem with Chopin is Mozart
and the problem with Dizzy Gillespie is Wynton Marsalis
and the problem with everything that has come since is
everything that came before. The problem with dying is everyone
does it in their own time and no one picks their own mahogany coffin.

VS. WORLD

If I were careening down Broadway dressed in my Sunday suit.
If my arms were out to either side, my hands extended.
If my eyes were shut, my head tilted.
If my coruscating smile, the kind you'd see in an advertisement.
If roses sloughed off my back and outstretched arms.
If streamers and ribbons followed, and the air seemed aglitter.
If the light fell such that no one in New York cast a shadow.
If I were followed by wolves and playful malamutes,
if the wolves wore velvet collars and the malamutes red kerchiefs.
If I spun.
If confetti in a million different colors from the skyscrapers.
If every window in Manhattan open, and the crowds roaring.
If the people on the curbs and streetcorners tried to reach out to me,
if they clapped, if they pointed, if they whistled.
If everyone on the streetcorners wore fedoras and bowlers,
if elbow patches on every coat.
If I were in slow motion, ecstatic, and trailed by wolves.
If the roses and rosepetals littered the streets behind me.
If all of Manhattan, made of rose petal.
If I had no one to share it with.
If I had no one I had to share it with.

untitled (10/31/09)

You stapled to your shirt to the mirror, said, "This is my costume, I am Narcissus." Anyone else could have thought of it but you did. You must be a genius, you must be part medusa, part laugh, part werewolf, unicorn, wonder woman, constantly shifting guises and tricking folks into thinking this is by far the orangest night of the year and all the sugar in the children's bags is just an experiment of luck and harvest, of weather, shift and tide, of charm.

what is for real and what is for sure

Midnight, your
birthday. Your father
sent a roll of quarters.
We can go do laundry
or walk on down
to the bar/arcade.
The moon is a riot.
Colors come down
like curtains.
Silver. Orange. Blue.
The radio stays awake
with old college rock
tunes. Call in, request
your favorite song. What
language? OK means zero
killed. The soldiers say
it is so on other radios.
The barracks shape up
like dorm rooms do.
Smelling of socks, how
some boys do—
oh, boys—oh, boys.
We skipped over cracks
on the sidewalk. We've
got our mothers' backs.

TEETH

You've never had nice teeth,
so you use them as a tools
to open beer bottles, or to cut thin wires.
In lieu of a toothbrush, you've used a knife.
Your father died with all his teeth,
brown and rotted to the gums.
You laugh loud with your mouth open.
At dinner, you smack your lips
while you chew. The woman
who loves you, frowns
when you show your large incisors.
Not as shy as your tongue,
yours face one another
fighting for the front space.

Megan Levad

PLEASE RELEASE ME

1. In my favorite picture of them

they're smiling, that is, she smiles
at the camera and he smiles at her
and they are young and beautiful
at a table in the yard with a long white cloth
for the dozens of aunts and uncles come
to see the baby. And I am the baby
and they are happy

2. Long ago, when there were wolves and whales

they saw each other in the courthouse square
she flashed black eyes

and a whole lotta collarbone
he wore an aviator's scarf and gray fedora

> and the Union soldier in the fountain
> saw the whole thing: his eyes on hers her eyes on his
> her oh, oh, here we go, there's no beach
> let's have them duck behind a red oak

> > people everywhere, her friends
> > waiting on the park bench, and still
> > she twists to let him. He feels the thump
> > of her breast, thick of her thighs

and a month later they marry.
She quit the squeaking one-room schoolhouse

and the Union soldier in his cement jacket
still couldn't get out of the water twenty-five years later
when their seventh son blacked him up
for the Fourth of July hog roast—seven sons all in a row

and according to the cheap wool carpet they did not once
push the twin beds together

their flame was hot enough to propel a man

across a drafty farmhouse bedroom

3. Babies

We came around the corner by the drinking fountains and all the girls with
babies
were standing there with their babies bouncing babies on hips babbling at
babies
staring at each other like stupid babies
and we were staring too and then Jason Slater flicked his black hair out of his
eyes and said
Don't have a baby. And if you do, don't bring it to school.

4. My husband gave me a black eye

she tells the ladies.
Yanking the electric blanket

out from its hospital

corners, he clocked her.

(They should never
let their daughters

make the bed.)
When she tells me, I'm surprised

he's been able to keep it
to Jesus Christ and Goddammit

lo, all these many years
together. He's never struck her

once, far as I know.

5. Banana seat

Hey girl,
ya wanna,
ya wanna
see? Wanna see?

Get to the point, she says.

Oh, I got a point.
Wanna see?

6. Big brothers

They get her to sit on

the round red

cushion, the one
with the sprung spring

poking up
right in the middle of it.

7. In the beginning

Spent his life in a home
a Mongolian idiot
now they call it Down's
teach them to make change
but for him: case of Pepsi
and a new clock radio every Christmas

They squeezed him when he cried
squeezed him til he fainted
and in his little cinderblock room
he forgot the tart cling
of the apple and what it whispered to him
before they swept it out

> *for a minute in the beginning*
> *you knew as much as anybody*

8. Our boys all got married the same day

Met those girls at the Jubilee
liked what they saw, what they squeezed

took them up to the counter and asked
How much.

      (one could tuck her feet behind her narrow white shoulders)
      (one could tie a cord of wood in knots with her tongue)
      (one was mean as a cat)

After the party
they blasted off to the moon

started a colony
of football-playing, poem-reciting
D-cupped swingbang jellyrollers

      (our daughters stayed on the farm)
      (stayed to pick dandelions, make wine)
      (stayed to ready us for winter)

9. Ooh, you so pretty and so sweet

and if any man say otherwise
you tell him
he a damn liar

10. World Book

Name this climate, the trees that live here. Dogs working, toy, the native dress
of Russia, mimicked with a blouse and dirndl from the spare room closet,
made for the 1970 State Fair, not worn once. Find manners between man,
human, male adult, and Man o' War, *racehorse, jellyfish.* Etiquette, table
settings for oysters, turtle soup. *Do not write "please R.S.V.P." as the please is*

implied by S'il Vous Plait.

Home: igloo, yurt, junk. Imagine life with the man from Tibet. Look for the dirty words. Be disappointed. Try the Greek myths. Someone has torn out Io. Leda's missing too. Solemnly page through cats of every shade and texture, come to cat & mouse, *traditional games.* Play it alone, boot after boot beaten through the dead March snow.

11. In his suitcase

they found a ski mask
a spool of twine
latex gloves
two condoms

12. Blessed art thou among women

Round and sleek as a setting hen
she runs her fingernail
between the table leaves
stays in the kitchen most days

keeps the kittens in a box
beneath the bed, keeps her crumbs
and grease in a cup

       she can take a punch

13. Not blood

The youngest showed up

        His sons are red and hairy
        wife took off on a fiery wheel

at the nursing home and told her

    You have no right to the farm

    Not blood
    Just the vessel
    for my father's children

    just a Pandora's box of usurers and whores

        He pulled all his teeth with a hammer,
        left the mouth-hole to rot

    And I cannot deny
    I count myself in that number, woman

14. The Teacher

You like this?
You like to pose for me, baby?

She arches, grinds her
knees into the coverlet,
leaves knee-prints in the chenille.

He reads them like tea
leaves in the morning:

You are lucky with money.
Careful traveller.
I see three children. Two or three.

15. By the time I got to choose

only toiletries remained: nail polish, pink
foam curlers, cold cream. I wanted

a bottle of foundation, Suntan
(though she was not outdoorsy,
as they used to say. She preferred
the kitchen table, a Virginia Slim
and cards to gardening).

It had separated, golden oil
floating over thick orange sediment. At the end,
they said, she didn't have the strength
to do more than worry on some
lipstick, crush scented powder to her neck

before she put on another pot of coffee
to greet the day's company.

16. We've got it all on film

and you can watch it on a cold sunny day in February
when you've spent too much time alone

drinking coffee til your veins feel scraped out

17. I was always a real little thing

Their song is
Pleeease release me, let me go—
I don't love you anymore

To waste our lives would be a sin

THERAPY

Winters I sleep more
to exist a little less.

I read once that even bits
of light, like the insect
eyes of electronics
on standby, make

for distracted sleep,
so I slip a slightly dirty
T-shirt over my face,

smell in its armpit
another version of what
I'm trying to sidestep:

acrid David.
Thanks, sleep.

My body's a weight
I place upon my body
to ease me out.

The lower I am, the quicker
the drop. I don't get why
the dark keeps what
I give it, and God
knows where it's kept.

Mostly, it works: I reemerge
mildly undepressed.

I just tossed this empty T-shirt on
the pillows to keep them from
resembling dented clouds.

LESSON

Teacher opened the door and Students stopped killing each other and tossed themselves into their corresponding desks. Teacher had an irritated look on. "How is it you children are so inefficient at killing one another? Every time I return, there you are tossing paper grenades, shouting empty threats, strangling each other in a theatrical manner. I suspect you lack conviction." Students sat there dumbly, chewing lower lips.
"Who taught you to carry on in such a way? Certainly not I..."
"The system and its comptrollers, as you've said."
"Oh, stuff the system. I never said such a thing—that was the book. Now look at how it's done." Teacher fetched the class gerbil from its dirty aquarium and wrung it like a wash towel.

"Teacher. Justice will find you out. Will justice find you out?"
"Don't be silly, that was only a demonstration. The world doesn't matter as much as you believe. Now open your books." Teacher tossed the wash towel back into the empty aquarium.

Tina Mozelle Harris

LONG BEFORE THE JFK GROUND CREW GATHERED AN ENTIRE BALE OF DIAMONDBACK TERRAPINS FROM THE TARMAC CLEARING THE WAY FOR GROUNDED JETS

"Turtles" appeared under "Infestation Types"
on restaurant health-inspection forms—proof
that somewhere waiters drifted out of the weeds

past the slow swim of the dishwashers.
Turtles skittered across the tiles, snatched bites
of lettuce from the lower shelves of the walk-in.

No one called out, "86 the terrapin" even when a lone
two-top lingered over dessert, coffee, nightcaps, so long
a turtle nudged a high heel—the woman squealed,

drew a foot into her chair. The turtle lifted its head and looked
the man in the eye. Their gaze grew taut between them,
both man and turtle slow to retreat to their homes.

THINGS I LEARNED FROM MY SONS WHILE DRIVING THEM HOME FROM SCHOOL

There is a religion in Vietnam that worships Charlie Chaplin and Victor Hugo.

Long Island has four McDonald's restaurants per square mile.

Mrs. Morris, the English teacher, swears.

The Great Wall is not the only man-made thing you can see from outer space.

A world famous violinist, whose concerts usually sell out at $100 a ticket, dressed as a bum and played Bach for 45 minutes in a Metro station. Only six people stopped to listen.

In Dubai there is a group of islands in the shape of a palm tree.

If you stand in the schoolyard during recess playing the theme from "Rocky" on a kazoo, you could earn $1.27 and a refrigerator magnet.

All girls look better with bangs. And makeup is the most disgusting invention. Ever.

You can't fold a paper in half more than eight times.

On the new Baskin-Robbins logo, a pink 31, for thirty-one flavors, is hidden in the BR.

A boy in seventh grade breeds guppies in his locker and sells them in water bottles.

Imagine a solid steel ball the size of the earth. A bird flies by and brushes its wing on the ball's surface once a year. When the whole ball has eroded, eternity is just beginning.

SAMPAGUITA

*Sampaguita (Philippine Jasmine) is
the national flower of the Philippines.*

The full sun does not singe
our soft five-petaled faces.
Nestled in the deep
gloss of leaves, we only
bloom more fiercely.

By night, our long-fingered
scent goes to your head.
Seeds? We have none.
Cut our slender stalks,
we multiply faster.

So we do not mind
when street children pluck
our immaculate buds, sew them
into wreaths for the dust-rimed
necks of your saints.

When you kneel to pray,
our perfume will soothe
whatever ails. You'll forget
how a girl, barefoot and empty-
bellied, tapped on the glass

of your air-conditioned car,
traded a rosary of whorled petals
for the coins in your pocket.

And when we open our diminutive
mouths to say, *our phosphorescence*

lights your moonless equatorial nights.
what we mean is, you will not
find us in the morning,
unless the wind has dropped
our withered tunics in your path.

LAVENDER

Color of baby rooms and funeral parlors,
of handkerchiefs and lotions and corsages and dried
flowers. That peculiar scent of something intimate
being made clean or covered up. Bathroom air
fresheners. Perfume after sex. Petals 'round the corpse.
I have smelled it all my life, like anyone
in my tribe, in this time, and have never noticed just how
embarrassing it is. Like an overzealous mother.
And the oddness of its spelling, the way the V
comes down and hatchets the ender
into a mutter. Gives Lav all the strength,
an evocation of *love* rather than *dead ends.*
This awful color-slash-scent, pale and pink and slow,
reminiscent of a fatal skin condition,
is ready for scars. In the shopping aisle, in soap
and shampoo and make-up, salves and powders and balms.
Cools the skin with deathly creeping quick. Massaged
across flesh and into pores and crevices
the way any skilled mortician would— and will.
Just to keep us calm for the sweet-smelling crypt.

DRIVING WEST

One last wave, the awkward promises to call
or write, then the waves of rain and snow, road salt
and spilled coffee cresting on the highways.

I keep saying goodbye to the mirrors, the faces
of strangers there, the drooped flesh and stooped brow
on my own irrelevant self staring back. In each state

there are tolls to pay. No one will listen to me
singing to myself about the road-gray skies,
making up words for a tune I just barely recall.

So I scan the fuzz instead: Famous lovers split, Liberals
spit on America, lots are filled with low-priced cars,
and I could drive for days. I might not ever quit.

Strange country, I'm but a character you imagine;
you are real. I bend my limbs to your landscape's verbs.
If I'm alive, it's only because you dreamt me.

LILIES

If the stacks of paper on your dining room table
are correct, you're about to buy your first house.
Those many stacks of paper full of numbers,
photos, and warnings: of bugs chewing up the beams,
of wires fraying. The papers are saying that the garden
is old and overgrown, they give advice and dimensions

but fail to note the statue of St. Francis in the ivy,
the small grotto you found drowning in nasturtiums
last Sunday when you drove there after church
and trespassed, walked through that backyard as if
it were already yours, and made big plans.
The stacks of paper on your big dining room table

don't take into account whether that table
will fit in the new dining room. And so you stay up
late at night trying to remember things: how the light
slants down though the trees, and what's beyond
that big picture window with its sloppily painted sills.
The stacks of paper on your dining room table

congratulate you for a fine interest rate
but, spoiled child, you're thinking instead
Hurrah for hardscaping!
Hurrah for electricity in the old garage!
Hurrah for the jade plant holding up the black mailbox!
Spoiled child, you're thinking of what you should pull out first

to make room, to set the yard perpetually in bloom,
and what more you'll buy: four kinds of climbing roses,
five kinds of lilies. You're thinking of yourself, and how
you've been so fearfully and beautifully made
to know all about drywall and planter boxes.
Maybe one of these nights you'll think

how lilies are beautiful and get so little done.
And look at your own finery. And dial back your plans.

HISTORY OF ANGELS

Where angels meet him
the brightest fell. 1842.
All of them wild. March
morning I hear angels wail. 1858.
Penitents' tears
the wine angels pour. 1865.
1611. Everlasting fire
prepared for the angels.
1717. Bright clouds descending.
Angels watch round.

1875. Angel of innocence
vanished. Angel of repentance
takes him gently by the hand.
1808. Ministering angel: Thou.
1860. Announces things of God
to the people. 1879.
Last utterance of the angel,
Malachi. 1831.
Until I fulfill the angel's command
to fast. 1637.

Dear good angel of spring. 1853.
Father summoned by the angel.
1855. Angel carved in stone
weeps over her. Soaks her blouse.
1719. Angel of money fall. 1808.

Scatter angel's food across the court.
1943. Gather angels together. 1967.
Echoes. Dubbed angels. Echoes.
Song of birds in migration.

OPEN AIR TOMB

"Excuse my dust."
— *Dorothy Parker*

The living shed and flake,
can't fake or hide
the brown powdery slough
seasoning every home. The past
has quite a will to live,
recycled as dry mist, as tickle
at the back of a throat or speck
in your eye. Earth's daily grind
is full of circumplanetary bits
looking to settle—disintegration
carries its own far-flung secrets,
cause and effect as physical drift,
everyone's incognito motes
part of the enduring crumble.

2/7 WHO WRITES POEMS ABOUT THE SPECULUM OF HENS

Of all the Body and Soul Ballads I inherited from my father,
I wonder which one was his favorite. Here I am again
speaking of a song that spoke to him sincerely. I meant,
son. Speaking of how I spoke to him about the pendulum
that clocks the speculum in my ear like a metronome
clocks a beat beneath a rap song. Spoke to him about her
and how she crawls around inside my body
like a dirty south ditty before camping out
in coronary position where my hand is on my heart
pledging to all that she is. I hoped he'd say, "She likes
to inspect," that way I could imagine her in my head
leading me on, that way I could ignore the feathers I lost
from plumage I used in a second attempt. What he said
offered no chorus of men in our bloodline nor clarity
in the mirror of me looking deep within myself for a song.

2/24 DUNG BEETLES

Grubs recycle dung. Can't think of shit else to say
about that, save garbology in the hands of A.R. Ammons,
mirrors the muddled reflection of my face
in a candy bar wrapper tossed on the floor
by my nephew who has a sweet tooth for chocolate
as long as my worm for books. We live in
what we waste—we live through denial. Outside of
the box of gourmet popcorn, into the core of an apple
energy bends to recycle matter. The grub,
unlike the alchemist, gets its lamellae clicking
like strike anywhere matches, picks up the pungent
smell of sulfur while overturning shit we refuse to burn.

Vievee Francis

"THE WORLD CONTRACTS"
−Zagajewski

Sip a sweet cordial and the lonely stars grow closer,
lean forward, so unlike biting into a lemon
all yellow and pith. Bite into that
and on the other side of the city a man will yell,
"What the hell's in my eye?"
Like yesterday, I saw the smoke of a fire
from the highway, I couldn't figure the miles,
it seemed close to my house (which is a flat
above a shop but I call it home) and I drove
faster and faster to save it, my house, from
the flames I knew were below the smoke,
but when I got there, there was no fire
just smoke wafting from the belching incinerator
ten miles further on. Still, the smoke was there,
the stink of waste. What is distance
but the leap from womb to light, from light
to dark again. I toast the gazelle
whose flesh nourishes the lion
I watch on television, so close I fear it,
but don't turn away. What difference
lies between birth-slap and cry? Between
our eating and any other grind?
I go out into the night and throw up my arms
as if to pull toward me every unknown thing.

THE LIBRARIAN

Over years my mother collected a library of pins,
pins with which to startle a balloon, tuck a hat,
pinion the legs of a frog,
prick a daughter suspected of witchcraft.
With her prizes she could read my future,
throwing them down on the ground like blanched chicken bones,
spilling them into the bottoms of paper cups.
So much nicer than needles, pins,
with their capped tops, or hooks,
nothing to get lost under the skin.
There was a doll in a drawer that looked like me,
an expression equally dark, my father's face,
with an unsmiling mouth and an unrestrained nose.
It had a hundred tiny holes.
I was born sickly and remain so.
I walk through the library and can't help but be impressed.
The work of years evident, cool,
silver as the gleam in a narrowed eye.

Vievee Francis

NEAR THE END OF THE TALE

Consider – the prongs of the fork,
the cup and ladle, the chipped creamer,
the sweating walls, the fire's log,
the chimney rising above chocolate roof,
the chair that squeaks as it rocks
with a sound mice make
when their tails are cut, the whining
teakettle, the catless windowsill,
and a three-skirted woman basting meat
in a dutch-oven, spooning fat over a haunch,
as the white bread rises on the tiles, and
a once small boy waits on his stool
for another bowl another bowl of this
or that, and thinks, how good
to be so free of hunger,
to be so warm inside.

106 | Another & Another

VISION

I tell the truth and no one believes,
or I speak in a tongue known only to me,
so I learn to say nothing, but
everyone talks because talking fills the hours
and the silence over meals, and days.
I put my truth to bed: say,
hush darling, sleep,
and the nights pass into years.
My truth and I have gray streaks
but don't consider this a sign
of wisdom. I was awakened by a kiss,
but my truth sleeps on.
Soon, we will both be wrinkled,
but only I will have been loved.

Richard D. Allen

DON'T KILL YOURSELF AT THE OFFICE

don't kill yourself at the office
it doesn't have a payoff
it's not like your boss
is going to have to clean it up

he won't be cradling
your lifeless body
saying this was once a man
we are all guilty

some janitor is going to find you
later that night he's going to say
to himself or his wife
in some diphthong-heavy language

I have seen a terrible thing
don't ask me to provide any details
I'm just going to try to block it out
what am I going to do, quit?

I checked, the suicide
had more money in his wallet
than I could spend in a month
I suspect witchcraft

kill yourself in a city park
many of them are quite lovely
and if you choose your location carefully
you can almost ensure

you'll be found by a jogger
we all hate joggers don't we
let's see you keep to your
sub-seven-minute-mile pace

with a dead executive
lying in your path
you sinewy asshole
seriously though don't kill yourself

if you have to quit, quit
if you're going to be fired, quit
if you've been fired, say
you can't fire me, I quit

commit career suicide
destroy yourself
in the sense of who you once were
not in the sense of all you are

you might not get unemployment
but you won't rot in the ground
which sounds more fulfilling
cracking your skull with a bullet

or running through the office
shouting obscenities
being chased by security
throwing your papers

from the mezzanine
watching them descend
on the crowd
in a cool white rain

Karyna McGlynn

FIONA APPLE (AMERICAN MUSICIAN, 1977–)

In a world where only Fiona Apple knows what's wrong with the water.
In a world where Fiona Apple and a lowly French horn
                  must traverse post-apocalyptic Delaware.
In a world where Fiona Apple is my babysitter forever & ever.
In a world where Fiona Apple & Fatty Arbuckle make love on the terrace.
In a world where Fiona Apple & the Blue Meanies attack Pepperland.
In a world where Fiona Apple & Paul Thomas Anderson
                  fashion the world's first sex sling.
In a world where Fiona Apple is the secret behind holistic medicine.
In a world where Fiona Apple is the slum-lord of my brown, brown duplex.
In a world where Fiona Apple makes titles long, irrelevant train tracks
                  on which nothing beautiful can ever grow again.

METAMORPHOSIS/MINOR SUIT/MILITARISM

A man tries to teach you and everyone you know Euchre. The rules are delirious and immense, and everyone is too full of chicken and marijuana to take the game seriously. Even worse, it's a patriotic themed deck, and everyone is pretty sure this somehow factors into play. The man reveals the rules incrementally so as not to overwhelm. This doesn't work very well. As soon as everyone thinks they've got it, getting in that smooth groove like, "I am Master of the Euchre Universe," the rules change. Players with jokers have to trade hands, or trade seats. Players with more than twelve cards have to sit on their hand, while players with fewer than six cards have to count to ten in German before discarding. But only on odd numbered minutes, unless you have an 'S' in your name. It's possible you're remembering some of this wrong. This is why, when the floor starts rolling like the muscles under the ribs of a heaving dog, it takes everyone too long to realize what's happening. Everyone thinks: *wow, too much white wine and pot and chicken. I'd better go lie down.* But then, an unfortunate ceramic butterfly falls off Tim's knick-knack shelf and crashes operatically to the floor. You look at each other sarcastically like 'okay, *who* started the *séance*?' But then Black Heather (who's not black) (but who is from California) says, simply: *Earthquake. Everybody get in a doorway.* But there aren't enough doorways for you and everyone you know, so some people get in the bathtub, and other people get under the bed. Somebody says, "It's not a tornado, morons." But nobody's sure *what* it is. It's Tim's apartment but it's being kneaded by a giant rolling pin. Much later, the man will tell you that this was the night you truly became an adult—with the president on the television looking gravely disingenuous—talking about some other abstract concern that had nothing to do with the earthquake in Seattle. It's funny to imagine now: your brain sapped of its vestigial baby fat. You were twenty-seven. You don't remember any of the rules leading up to or including the night you learned Euchre.

FREAK

With his pearl handled cane,
the sideshow barker has all day gestured

for the Midway gadabouts—
shoving handfuls of popcorn in their

already full mouths—to step inside
the painted tarp that promises a man

not quite a man, & so tonight, they watch
me wrestle with a fork,

a platter of spaghetti. I know this burden—
with only a thumb & little finger—

will prove difficult to raise to
my lips, yet my mouth insists

on its mad rake, its queer tongue
wags in the air as if

this fork won't slip
through these cleft hands—

with their hold-that-is-not-a-hold.
Eventually, I'll stoop or crawl

on all fours—as I often do—
as the popcorn eaters howl,

slap their knees at the audacity
of such hunger,

point their buttered fingers
at these phantom ones that grapple

for the silver handle,
its bent tines—

bent not from some splendid gnash,
but this constant disaster—gesture

in every direction, always deciding who eats
what & how &

like the much anticipated
punchline of a joke, I

pick up the fork with my
toes, laugh my laugh-that-is-not-a-laugh.

Tommye Blount

TEETERING ON ONE FOOT,

I slipped the other in my mother's
open toe heels.

I know how this is done,
the treacherous step
                    down the arch

a boy must take, all this weight

balanced on the ball of my
foot

here where her toes
once gathered at the tapered edge.

I fetch the pearls—
they cross my thin throat

once more than hers—then shuffle
to the ransacked closet, slip inside

the yellow dress—
in which tomorrow

she'll be buried—
then wrestle with the zipper,

this notion of closure.

I look back
into the dresser's mirror, find my mother

staring back.
I grab a tube of lipstick

glide it across
our mouth.

MOSTLY TO UNCOVER THE REALITY OF MY DESTRUCTIVE HUNGER

He gave me nothing to eat but photographs of other people eating meat. Cooked and raw, half-gone and about to be sliced. In the photographs the people looked relaxed and not very hungry. But first they were killing the animals with their careful machines. This was before clumsy hands came to the collective mauling. And before the children danced carefully in their ironed clothes at their little table. It all looked delicious. The shiny weapons and thick spats of flesh and slavering mouths and families. He did this in order. In order that I might see how feeding is done.

MOSTLY TO UNCOVER THE REALITY OF MY CLOSED FIST

He pressed needles between my fingers to see if I would bleed, and I did. Bled through the tiny pricks. Tiny red dots that didn't spill, torn tracks of skin. Needle hitting bone. Prick. Prick, prick. Fingernails made crescents deep into the supple yellow mount of my palms. I kept moving. Near Vine, wavering palm trees bent toward dirty streetshops but didn't touch. People walked on stars and spat gum, phlegm. Flashed new tattoos and private piercings. Held hands. Some held needles in their arms or a memory. I pressed tighter, closed my mouth around my teeth. My closed hands made two needled fists. They bled from their infant pores. I couldn't feed them, couldn't stroke them, couldn't give them up.

(purification: wolf moon)

O

I stood in the earth's skull & swept
my fur skirts clean, I grew tall
& taller, shed the dust,
shed supple hunch, crown of wild
dandelion & ate it; humid breath
stretched my weedy neck & bent
my arms into scythes: blue-tongued
& sharp-mouthed, I stood
between beasts & thorn trees & waited:

O

I heard a howling, but did not run
I heard a howling, but did not run
I heard a howling, but did not run

i dare you to remember

your body. the spandexed breastbone, worked to a shine. where the lungs sit in the middle
of the floor and howl to gods. name that bird out the north window, i

dare you. the south star getting hotter. what it takes to be a bad buddha. a watery
way of the rock. your native jokes slip down sweat into meatless folds. you have

the whitened teeth of a new age beaver. your spittle collecting rainbows over prayers
to sun, i bet. you are killing birds at one time. another sweater notices

you suck in your gut. or throw two stones. some have already wished your pores
would close up. but you, your commercials are shot. there are helicopters in the desert

waiting with meal trays. maybe even
fowl. the rest

dig at tiny holes in the hot tents, hunting
air.

francine j. harris

whenever anyone says no

walk backwards. stand on your head. change the wind
and uncrook all the mouths that bitter

to a time once when someone the color of wet tea, of 1976, of twirling
benches
inside coney islands with hands sturdy around your ankles, perched you high

above his head of tinted, sunlit hair and dodged the low hung branches, as
the city spun, the bus stops

and black birds and faded phone wires.
an ash of afternoon.

what carried you then
as now
lifts the sheets from your eyes, balances
sun from sand with the noise of brown pigeons

alight the rose brush drying at the end of summer.

all the rules

if you ever   balanced a dish   on your forehead
you might think   this were rather   simple to say
easy to loosen   the lips over   metronomes. phrases and
    delicately stacked idioms.   still somehow, it
seems things get
thrown off or   overdone, sometimes. my   mouth's crooked.
notice?
    or my pants   are stuck again.   or the
glue
didn't take. do   you ever find   yourself cheating
(in) games
          you made up?   like, you know all the rules,
    and if it   were someone else   man, they would
so call foul.   blue, chewy verbisms.   sticky, swampy
articles.
          you remember because   they are stuck
in your eyeball.
                    i mean, duh.
    you could admit   there're some things   (does that work?)
you can't account   for being unable   to say.
fairly.

francine j. harris

the way i remove clothes

is a window. a sawmill, with the blade
exposed. there are hundreds of violet trees

through stuck raindrops. like a chokechain.
all the way there, the tires. too much air

between words. too many winds of road
where there could have been cliff guards, a metallic

you'd know by taste. there are no such exits, when stutter.
when stripped. when ditches take the driver.

give up in the mud. where the west lay ahead and sideswiped.
lipstick on the dash. maybe blood. down a hill, a lumberyard

and a worker in overalls. is cutting wood
for a new barn. a different horse

than the one he knows.

YOU

I see you with your arm up to your elbow in the candy machine, cussing and screwing your lips. I see you and a fleck of spit lands in the space between us when you tell me good morning. I see you digging the grit from the corner of your eye. I see you lying down under your unwashed comforter, rolling onto your stomach, alone at last. I see you pause on the station with a picture of the missing child. I see you beautiful in your sleep as you trail a leopard in perfect silence with the grace you were meant to have. I see you delighted at your own genius when you discover a pair of dimes and a couple of quarters in the ash tray, enough to buy a chocolate bar for breakfast. I see you thinking of the girl who stands in front of you at the coffee machine; she has a nice ass. I see you as your heart beats. I see you with your gorgeous neck, still smelling of shaving cream. I see you hungry. I see your fingers twitch. I see you naked in darkness.

Mary Jo Thompson

NIGHT JAR

On the roof tonight
tears garnish my throat.
I can't scream like the nighthawks,
but silently admire
how they cross the wind
in spiro gyro flight.
I used to fear they might be
bats. That they'd bite
or want to tangle hair.
Saw them both careen
with mouths agape,
suck up flying insects
like black holes swallow stars.
Now I know that neither
wants to come down here.
They don't rob nests.
Won't roost and shit
like doves. May god love most
those who help us
though we want to do them harm.

AGAINST PRECISION

Yesterday I stumbled upon a wreckage of beauty. White blossoms clouded an unnamed tree and uncountable petals from its simple flowers dotted the ground. Sitting down inside the heavy smell, I named the tree "mock orange." No one would care. With this gesture I admitted how it felt good to be inaccurate. The rock near my foot, dirt covered, dirt colored, of lethal weight, potato-sized, had a place for my thumb. I called it "Killer." The river came over its banks like a piece of silk ripped by knives. It would be "consort." Naming things became easier as time wore on.

Matthew Poindexter

LOVE POEM WITH FALSE RABBIT AND HOUSE KEY

No one buys a faux-stone rabbit for themselves:
when locked out of the house,
they simply reach beneath the doormat,
the potted plant. At my last place
it was the loose brick in the walkway,
unwedged to find the spare
sealed in a sandwich bag.

Yet yesterday at Lowe's, I stopped
at shelving overrun with plastic rabbits,
birds, and squirrels, machine-molded
so their insides could be used
for hiding keys. Each felt too light
and looked too cheap to safeguard
everything I own, much less
for thirty bucks apiece, their paint jobs
little more than small dull dots:
some grey, some black, some brown specks
splattered on their empty bodies.

But what they're hollowed out to harbor
made me think of you, of us.
The idea of our brass codes clanging
in your purse as you walk to church
or when you swipe your frequent shopper card
across the scanner at the grocery store—
somehow I can't bring myself to make a key

that's yours outright. For now, you'll find
a copy in the faux-stone rabbit waiting
on his haunches by my door. Make sure
no one sees you. Let yourself in.

Matthew Poindexter

OFF-DAY ON THE HAW RIVER

I don't care that even though
I put the losing side of my new haircut
on the roses last night, the deer
still cleaned the stems by morning.

I don't care that she and I sleep
almost as if married now, which is both
good and bad. The same goes
for the ambiguity in its being both.

I don't even care that the all-star game,
in all its false wholesomeness,
is on TV tonight, and my team might win
for the first time in twelve years.

Light is dyeing the sheet of river
slipping down the spillway orange
and I just lifted a small dun turtle
out of the shallows. I keep it warm

in my open palm. When it unshells itself
there thirty minutes later, the pane
of water is back to being brown,
my team is five runs down, she and I

still seem strange and the deer are hungry
again. But in my hand, something feels

more cared for than before. At least
one small wish I make gets granted.

Matthew Poindexter

RECLAMATION DAY

I come today to reclaim my grandmother's clothesline,
acknowledged last in nineteen-ninety-nine, when I was twelve,
when James said only trailer trash don't got a dryer.

I'd never seen it that way before—yet in his hurtful jab
work shirts transformed to flags, signaling WE ARE POOR
for all to see. It stopped existing then, far easier for me

to stay away from her back yard, to sit inside and watch TV
when we would visit on those Sundays after church.
My grandmother's clothesline: two lengths of cord wound taut

between two poles, to me forever linked with *y'all*
and modern country radio—a trinity abandoned,
now in the process of some slow return.

Today, I come to reclaim, to take back
that which once was good to me, a prodigal son
not asking for a fatted calf, but just a place to dry his clothes.

So much from youth deserves its exile on the Isle
of My Embarrassment: a "Blame It On The Rain" cassingle
backed with "Girl You Know It's True," my penchant

for those ultra-wide-legged jeans with umpteen pockets—
complete with faux-gang logos—sagging off my ass.
The bongo drums I bought to match my RASTA! poster.

Her clothesline never should have been lumped in with them,
imbecilic fads that lack the line's utility. What caused
my childish shame, the line, was never close to being wrong.

It is the shame itself I now regret. Let me undo
that wooden pin. Let me put that stiff and faded shirt
on my back now, and give her line less weight.

Dara Barnat

EARLY MARRIAGE POEM

We probably got married
just this past June. My veil was lifted
by the wind, and we said blessings:
mekudeshet, mekudeshet, mekudeshet.
My mother cried and my father
was probably not there, because he died
after years in a hospital.
Your mother also cried, while your father stood
to the side of the congregation,
probably not revealing too much
on his face, as always.

I know you're scared to have children,
but we'll probably have a child,
and you'll carry this child in your arms,
like your friend from high school carried
his little girl at the party we went to
over the weekend, as if she were a sparkly gift,
wrapped in a red corduroy dress.
This is what fatherhood can be,
I probably thought, at its best. I believe
you have it in you to deliver that kind of love.

And I'll probably be faithful to you,
which is probably inadequate faithfulness,
because I find it hard to resist attraction,
and I'm not sure I won't give in

now and again. You'll probably
be faithful to me. I imagine us in forty years,
a breeze over our bodies at night.

A miracle in and of itself, to be breathing
the same air, until one day we probably won't.

Karen Llagas

DESCENT

My mother's name means *end*
in Tagalog and my father's name
means *wound* in Spanish.

The prepositions I must supply
—in, until, of, despite—
or perhaps a clause—and?

Asked to explain my melancholy
I offer my full name and continue
to reside in English.

To be a daughter is to have
a duty to grammar, to exact
the relationship between

words that otherwise disappear
into *vision—super*, then lack of,
and much later, *di—*

In the family albums everyone
is always held by someone else,
in siesta or in fiesta.

My mother's young
legs looked miraculous and
the caption said so—legs!

A man in bell-bottoms
turned up in a portrait with a look
that means defiance,

or father. Back turned
on the house, his shadow
formed the perfect *I* on the ground.

MAPLE WING

A body wishes to be held and held and what
can you do about that?

II. The Father
Because, I suppose, being human,
we know when best to ask another
to continue their obligation to us
to live. The patient's wife said he
looked happy days before he died,
so she told him, *you're getting*
better, let's go home tomorrow.
Suppose that Jesus answered No.
No to the drunkards in the temple,
and to the pockets noisy with coins,
no to Mary Magdalene, to her
almond-scented hair, no to the sponge
soaked with vinegar, no to the sand.
Father gave us everything we
asked for. Always a yes, the patient's
daughter said, during the wake.
Can't you hear, I wanted tell her—
so soft, you might have missed it—
right here, solid the way only
horizontal is, his smoothed face,
his starched suit, he's telling you, *No.*

AMERICA

In the middle of Omaha,
chasing a man, I know that it's you

many years now, many nights.
Your beautiful blankness
that is the sky when no one
is looking at it. The lakes you've
made of our mouths.
        America, I want your brand
of ecstasy bursting
in me like champagne.

I want that power
to exempt from suffering

whomever I deem worthy
with only a few syllables,

a name, a self so solid
it gives off rays
as if made of glass.

MISCARRIAGE

It plays out differently in my dreams every night. This time
I am walking through gardens of newborns.
I'd rather look at the butterflies than the human infants—
they're the prettiest coming up: big blooms
like tissue paper that open as the sun rises, close tight
when it sets. I sit down in the garden's center.
The butterfly to my left is especially pretty, especially thin,
so the late afternoon light filters through
onto my hand, turning it stained glass for a moment.
Still, I am drawn to where the humans
are growing. The smell is like soup broth, and my pants
keep getting caught on the thorny things
that circle the little hands sticking up from the ground
in irregular patches. Most of them
are clenched tight, like tiny fleshy potatoes.
I look for hands that have opened,
palms up. I pass by dozens before I am stopped
by one near a tree, hardly stunning:
five fingers, rosy, knuckles in the right places.
I grab hold to pull it from the soil
but it pulls back, harpooning me down,
down, until I am swallowed
by the warm hollow of roots and legs,
all tangled together.

LIKE DINOSAURS

They'll find us in the mud.
First the brush will uncover
your femur, dusting away
the remaining hunks of the last
eighty-or-so million years,
those eons of fossilized sludge
packed on top of us. Next
will be my ribs and vertebrae,
jumbled as tangram pieces.
Mistaking us for one animal,
they'll name their discovery
Duocranion, string us up
in a nice arrangement,
legbones knocking
like wind chimes.

HYDROPHOBIA

but now I notice everything. My sink
holds a sea, overflows, becomes a

waterfall, becomes
a puddle at my feet. I notice

towels make no effort to intervene,
the floor is a willing participant.

I notice mildew, faint
but slowly owning the hallway carpet.

An article on waterboarding,
magazine pages grimed together. Notice

condensation on the living room window,
country-sill-cool, the beads

of moisture take solitary journeys
to the edge of the frame.

There is an icicle
on the other side of the locked door

taking its time to drill a tunnel
into a mound of snow, one drop

at a time. I'm noticing my hands,
how little they hold. They are teacups

bailing out a vessel not worthy of any sea
and silence is a rag

stuffed into the mouth
of a gurgling drain.

Jamaal May

IF THEY HAND YOUR REMAINS TO YOUR SISTER
IN A CHINESE TAKEOUT BOX

Think of the environment.
Ceramics aren't biodegradable
so if you want to be buried
in the plot with your estranged wife,
an urn won't do. You need to feed
the worms, play your role
in nurturing soil and lift
trees into the sky.

If your obituary is scrawled
on notebook paper, ripped out
and photocopied, rigid
edges and all. If the lines
still show through, faint
like soap scum collected
on the mirror above the sink
you were found slumped under.
If your girlfriend only showed up
to your motel room to find you
after a three-week absence
because your check came on the first.

If they hand your remains to your sister
in a Chinese takeout box. Take solace
in the laughter of your niece. Take solace
in the fact that you've torn

a liquor-stenched wound
down the middle of this family
and for once
it won't be mentioned as they gather.
Take solace because the bag
that carried you to the cemetery
will not go into the ground with you.
It will remain for decades
holding hands with a breeze,
wandering around a landfill
repeating in bold red font,

THANK YOU
THANK YOU
THANK YOU
THANK YOU
THANK YOU

ACKNOWLEDGMENTS

"Evening in Mendocino," "Dear Masoom," and "Thinking of His Jaywalking Ticket While Boarding a Plane at SFO" by Dilruba Ahmed were reprinted from *Dhaka Dust* with permission from Graywolf Press, copyright 2011.

"Dear Masoom" by Dilruba Ahmed previously appeared in *Catamaran: South Asian American Writing*.

"Thinking of His Jaywalking Ticket While Boarding a Plane at SFO" by Dilruba Ahmed previously appeared in *New England Review*.

"At the End of Life, A Secret" by Reginald Dwayne Betts previously appeared in *New England Review* and was reprinted in *Best American Poetry 2012*, edited by Mark Doty.

"Boundary Line" by Tamiko Beyer previously appeared in *Poemeleon*.

"sweet branch stitched to bitter tree" by Tamiko Beyer previously appeared in *Diagram*.

"Dream: the disappeared lover" by Ching-In Chen previously appeared in *Drunken Boat*.

"Chinese Workers at USDA Lab, 1904" by Ching-In Chen previously appeared in *The New Sound*.

"American Syntax" by Ching-In Chen previously appeared in *So to Speak*.

"Enough Time" by Nicelle Davis previously appeared in *Mosaic*.

"Long before the JFK Ground Crew Gathered an Entire Bale of Diamondback Terrapins from the Tarmac Clearing the Way for Grounded Jets" by Tina Mozelle Harris previously appeared in *Jellybucket*.

"Please Release Me" by Megan Levad previously published by the Poetry Center of Chicago.

"If They Hand Your Remains to Your Sister in a Chinese Takeout Box" by Jamaal May previously appeared in *The Collagist*.

"Fiona Apple (American Musician, 1977-)" by Karyna McGlynn previously appeared in *SIR! Magazine*.

"Open Air Tomb" by Sally Molini previously appeared in *Southern*

California Review.

"Engine in the Shape of a Tiny Metal Dog" by Matthew Olzmann previously appeared in *Salt Hill.*

"Sir Isaac Newton's First Law of Motion" by Matthew Olzmann previously appeared in *New England Review.*

"Torque" by Matthew Olzmann previously appeared in *H-NGM-N.*

"Mostly to uncover the reality of my destructive hunger" and "Mostly to uncover the reality of my closed fist" by Khadjiah Queen were reprinted from *Black Familiar* with permission from Noemi Press, copyright 2011.

"Mostly to uncover the reality of my destructive hunger" by Khadjiah Queen previously appeared in *Squaw Valley Review.*

"(purification) wolf moon" by Khadjiah Queen previously appeared in *wicked alice* and was reprinted by the Poetry Society of America (poetrysociety.org).

"Things I Learned from My Sons While Driving Them Home from School" by Angela Narciso Torres previously appeared in *The Collagist.*

"It was easier to manage" by Arisa White previously appeared in *The Minnesota Review.*

"Modern Problems" by Ross White previously appeared in *Waccamaw.*

"Vs. World" by Ross White previously appeared in *New England Review.*

"briar patch" by Laurie Saurborn Young previously appeared in *Southeast Review.*

"the making of history" by Laurie Saurborn Young previously appeared in *New South.*

Dilruba Ahmed's debut book of poems, *Dhaka Dust* (Graywolf, 2011), won the 2010 Bakeless Prize for poetry. Ahmed's writing has appeared in *Blackbird, Cream City Review, New England Review,* and *Indivisible: Contemporary South Asian American Poetry.* A graduate of the M.F.A. Program for Writers at Warren Wilson College, Ahmed teaches in Chatham University's Low-Residency M.F.A. Program. www.dilrubaahmed.com.

Richard D. Allen is a poet and humorist. He edits IRL LOL (irllol.com), a literary humor website. He lives outside Chapel Hill, North Carolina, with his wife, Belle Boggs.

Larissa Vidal Amir doesn't know how to write poetry. She earned an M.F.A. in Fiction from the M.F.A. Program for Writers at Warren Wilson College and tends to write stories shorter than this bio. Her work appears in *New Sudden Fiction* (Norton), *CRATE, Fiction at Work, The Portland Review,* and *eye~rhyme.* Larissa serves as an assistant editor for *Narrative.* She lives in Seattle with her wonder boy, Leo, and works as a financial analyst, but won't admit it.

Mark Andres is a visual artist, filmmaker and writer living in Portland, OR. His work has appeared in *Paragraph, Clackamas Literary Review,* and *Conduit.* He is the recipient of a Massachusetts Artist's Fellowship and an Oregon Literary Arts Grant. His work is represented by Augen Gallery of Portland. www.paintingintime.com

Dara Barnat's poetry appears or is forthcoming in *Poet Lore, Crab Orchard Review, Salamander, Flyway, The Collagist,* and elsewhere. Her chapbook *Headwind Migration* was released by Pudding House Publications in 2009. She has received a poetry work-study scholarship from the Bread Loaf Writers' Conference. Dara teaches poetry and creative writing in the

Department of English and American Studies at Tel Aviv University. She recently completed her doctorate, *Walt Whitman and Jewish American Poetry*. Dara's blog, devoted to issues that arise while writing a collection of poems, can be found at mybookandi.wordpress.com.

Reginald Dwayne Betts is a husband and father of two young sons. In 2012, President Barack Obama appointed Mr. Betts to the Coordinating Council on Juvenile Justice and Delinquency Prevention. An award-winning writer and poet, Mr. Betts' memoir, *A Question of Freedom: A Memoir of Learning, Survival, and Coming of Age in Prison,* was the recipient of the 2010 NAACP Image Award for non-fiction. In 2010 he was awarded a Soros Justice Fellowship to complete *The Circumference of a Prison,* a work of nonfiction exploring the criminal justice system. In addition, Mr. Betts is the author of a collection of poetry, *Shahid Reads His Own Palm.*

Tamiko Beyer is the author of *bough breaks* (Meritage Press) and *We Come Elemental* (Alice James Books, forthcoming). She received her M.F.A. from Washington University in St. Louis, Missouri, where she was awarded a Chancellor's Fellowship. She is a former Kundiman Fellow and a contributing editor to *Drunken Boat.* She works as the Advocacy Writer at Corporate Accountability International.

A native of Detroit, **Tommye Blount** now calls Novi, Michigan home. He is an advertising graduate from Michigan State University and a Cave Canem alum. He has had work published in *The Collagist, Cave Canem XI* anthology, and *Upstreet.* He is the current Holden Scholar for Poetry in the M.F.A. Program for Writers at Warren Wilson College.

Jonathan Bennett Bonilla participated in Grinds in February 2008 and July 2010. He graduated from the M.F.A. Program for Writers at Warren Wilson College in 2010. Currently, he is a professor of Creative Writing at Gordon College.

Joshua Buursma teaches academic writing at George Washington University in Washington, D.C., and at the University of Maryland, College Park. He has a B.A. in Cinema and Photography from Southern Illinois University, Carbondale and an M.F.A. in Creative Writing from the University of Michigan, Ann Arbor, where he won a Hopwood Award. Born and raised in St. Joseph, Michigan, he now lives in Washington, D.C. His work has appeared in *The Meadowland Review* and elsewhere.

Zena Cardman is a freshly-minted Bachelorette of Science hailing from Chapel Hill, North Carolina. Her research has taken her to the Arctic, the Antarctic, and a handful of oceans and deserts in between. As an undergraduate she was Editor-in-Chief of *Cellar Door*, UNC's literary magazine, as well as *Tract*, a digest exploring the intersections of art and science. Cardman currently writes for theseamonster.net and her own website, xyzena.com. She hopes someday to become the Jacques Cousteau of outer space.

Amanda Carver is a graduate of the M.F.A. program at the University of Michigan. Currently, she is an RN in Chicago, Illinois.

Ching-In Chen is the author of *The Heart's Traffic* (Arktoi Books/Red Hen Press) and co-editor of *The Revolution Starts at Home: Confronting Intimate Violence Within Activist Communities* (South End Press). She is a Kundiman and Lambda Fellow, part of the Macondo and Voices of Our Nations Arts Foundation writing communities, and has been a participant in Sharon Bridgforth's Theatrical Jazz Institute.

Nandi Comer is currently pursuing an M.F.A. in Poetry and an M.A. in African American and African Diaspora Studies at Indiana University. She has received a Vera Meyer Strube Poetry Prize, as well as fellowships from Cave Canem and Callaloo. Her poems have appeared in *Callaloo, Third Coast, Muzzle* and *The Journal of Pan African Studies*. She is originally from Detroit, Michigan.

Originally from Utah, **Nicelle Davis** now resides in Lancaster, California, with her son J.J. She teaches at Antelope Valley College. Her book *Circe* has been released from Lowbrow Press, *Becoming Judas* is forthcoming from Red Hen Press in 2013, and *In the Circus of You* (a collaboration with Cheryl Gross) is forthcoming from Rose Metal Press in 2014.

Chiyuma Elliott is a Stegner Fellow whose work has appeared in the *African American Review, Callaloo, the Collagist, MARGIE, the Notre Dame Review,* and *TORCH.* A Cave Canem Fellow, she recently received a Ph.D. in American Studies from the University of Texas at Austin and an M.F.A. in Creative Writing from the M.F.A. Program for Writers at Warren Wilson College. She lives in Oakland, California, with her husband and two noisy dogs.

Vievee Francis is the author of *Horse in the Dark* (Northwestern University, 2012) and *Blue-Tail Fly* (Wayne State University, 2006).

Emily Kendal Frey is the author of *The Grief Performance* (Cleveland State University Poetry Center, 2011) as well as several chapbooks and chapbook collaborations. She lives in Portland, Oregon, where she hosts the New Privacy series.

francine j. harris has recent work appearing in *Rattle, Callaloo, Michigan Quarterly Review,* and is the author of the recent chapbook *between old trees.* She is a Cave Canem fellow, has been nominated for a Pushcart Prize, and is currently in a Zell Postgraduate Fellowship year at the University of Michigan. Her first collection, *allegiance,* was published in 2012 by Wayne State University of Press as part of the Made in Michigan series.

Tina Mozelle Harris is a student in the M.F.A. program at the University of Oregon. Her poems have appeared in a variety of journals including *Red Mountain Review, Santa Clara Review, PMS poemmemoirstory, StorySouth,* and the anthologies *Family Matters: Poems of Our Families* and *As Ordinary and Sacred as Blood: Alabama Women Speak.*

Jenny Johnson's poems have appeared or are forthcoming in *The Best American Poetry 2012, The Collagist, The Southern Review, Beloit Poetry Journal,* and *Blackbird.* She was the recipient of the 2011 Chad Walsh Poetry Prize, a scholarship to the Bread Loaf Writers' Conference, as well as a residency at the Kimmel Harding Nelson Center for the Arts. She earned her M.F.A. from Warren Wilson College. Currently, she is a Visiting Lecturer at the University of Pittsburgh.

Henry Kearney, IV is from Robersonville, North Carolina. He holds an M.F.A. from Warren Wilson College. His poems have appeared in places such as *New England Review, Boxcar Poetry Review, The Collagist, North Carolina Literary Review, The Cortland Review,* and *The Dead Mule School of Southern Literature.* He was awarded a 2011 Dorothy Sargent Rosenberg Poetry Prize.

Angela Kirby won prizes for poetry and short fiction while a B.A. student in Creative Writing at Duke University. First published in 2011, she has been Grinding since 2009.

Megan Levad's writing appears or is forthcoming in *Tin House, Fence, Granta Online, American Letters & Commentary, The Society for Curious Thought, textsound,* and *Spinning Jenny,* as well as the Everyman's Library anthology *Killer Verse.* She lives in Ann Arbor, Michigan, where she runs the visiting writers series for the University of Michigan.

Karen Llagas is a recipient of the second Filamore Tabios, Sr. Memorial Poetry Prize, and her first collection of poetry, *Archipelago Dust,* was published by Meritage Press in 2010. She has an M.F.A. in Poetry from the M.F.A. Program for Writers at Warren Wilson College and a B.A. in Economics from Ateneo de Manila. Also a recipient of a Hedgebrook residency and a Dorothy Sargent Rosenberg Poetry Prize, she lives in San Francisco, California, where she works as a Tagalog interpreter and instructor, and a poet-teacher with the California Poets in the Schools (CPITS).

Chloe Martinez holds the M.A. in Creative Writing from Boston University and the M.F.A. in Poetry from the M.F.A. Program for Writers at Warren Wilson College. Her poetry has appeared in *The Cortland Review, The Normal School,* and *The Collagist,* and has been nominated for a Pushcart Prize. She lives in Haverford, Pennsylvania, with her husband and daughter.

Jamaal May was raised by two auto workers in Detroit, Michigan, where he eventually taught poetry in public schools. After making a living as a self-taught poet and musician, Jamaal went on to publish two chapbooks, earn an M.F.A. from Warren Wilson College, and be featured in *Callaloo, Indiana Review,* and *Michigan Quarterly Review* among other journals, films, and broadcasts. He's the recipient of fellowships from Cave Canem, Callaloo, and Bucknell University where he was named the 2011-2013 Stadler Fellow. His first full-length collection, *Hum,* won the 2012 Beatrice Hawley Award and will be published in Fall 2013 by Alice James Books.

Karyna McGlynn is the author of *I Have to Go Back to 1994 and Kill a Girl,* winner of the Kathryn A. Morton Prize from Sarabande Books. Her poems have appeared in *Fence, Salt Hill, Columbia Poetry Review, Copper Nickel, Octopus,* and *Denver Quarterly.* Karyna received her M.F.A. from the University of Michigan, and is currently pursuing her Ph.D. in Literature and Creative Writing at the University of Houston. She serves as poetry editor for *Gulf Coast.*

Myron Michael's poetry has appeared online and in *Days I Moved Through Ordinary Sounds* (City Lights, 2009), *Nanomajority, Fourteen Hills, Harvard Review,* and *Toad Suck Review.* His chapbook *Scatter Plot* won the 2010 Willow Books Integral Music Chapbook Prize, and he is co-author of *Hang Man* (Move Or Die, 2010). He lives in the Bay Area where he curates HELIOTROPE, a monthly reading series.

Sally Molini co-edits *Cerise Press* (www.cerisepress.com). Her work has appeared in *American Letters & Commentary, Diagram, Beloit Poetry*

Journal, Denver Quarterly, and *Cimarron Review,* among others. She lives in Nebraska.

Victoria Bosch Murray's poetry has appeared in *American Poetry Journal, Field, Harvard Divinity Bulletin, Inch, Salamander, Tar River Poetry, The Cortland Review,* and elsewhere. Her chapbook of poems, *On the Hood of Someone Else's Car,* was published by Finishing Line Press in 2010. She is a contributing editor at *Salamander* and has an M.F.A. in Poetry from the M.F.A. Program for Writers at Warren Wilson College.

Matthew Olzmann's first book of poems, *Mezzanines,* was selected for the 2011 Kundiman Prize and is forthcoming from Alice James Books. His poems have appeared in *Kenyon Review, New England Review, The Southern Review* and elsewhere. He is the poetry editor of *The Collagist.*

Shann Palmer is a Texan living in Virginia. She has forthcoming work in *Poetry South* and the *2013 Poet's Market* and all over the internet.

Soham Patel has work forthcoming in *The Destroyer.* She currently lives in Pittsburgh, Pennsylvania.

Matthew Poindexter's work has been featured in the *Best New Poets* series and at *The Awl.* He lives in Carrboro, North Carolina.

Khadijah Queen is the author of *Conduit* (Black Goat/Akashic Books 2008) and *Black Peculiar* (Noemi Press 2011), which won the Noemi Book Award for poetry. Her work, four times nominated for the Pushcart Prize and winner of a 2011 Best of the Net Award, appears widely in journals and anthologies including *jubilat, Best American Nonrequired Reading* (Houghton Mifflin 2010), and *Villanelles* (Random House 2012). A Cave Canem and Norman Mailer Center fellow, she holds an M.F.A. in Creative Writing from Antioch University Los Angeles.

David Ruekberg lives near Rochester, New York, and teaches English in the International Baccalaureate program at Hilton High School. He received his M.F.A. from Warren Wilson College and has enjoyed a residency at Jentel Arts in Sheridan, Wyoming. Publications include *Yankee, Poet Lore, North American Review, 88, Mudfish, Comstock Review, Metazen,* and others.

Travis Smith is in the M.F.A. program at the University of Mississippi. His work has appeared in *Wag's Revue, Crazyhorse, Southern Cultures,* and *Carolina Quarterly.*

Rachel Berry Surles, former poetry editor for *FUGUE* and the *Carolina Quarterly,* has been published in *Washington Square, 32 Poems,* the *Worcester Review,* and others.

Sheera Talpaz is a graduate of the M.F.A. program at the University of Michigan, where she received a Hopwood Award in poetry. Her essays and poetry have appeared or are forthcoming in *The Rumpus, The Collagist, La Petite Zine, Drunken Boat,* and other journals.

Mary Jo Thompson's long poem "Thirteen Months" is included in *Best American Poetry 2011.* Other work has been published in the *Beloit Poetry Journal, Indiana Review, Carolina Quarterly, Great River Review, Minnesota Poetry Calendar, Poetry Motel, North Coast Review, Sow's Ear Poetry Review,* and *Minnesota Monthly,* among other journals. She has collaborated with textile artist Mary Hark to create public installations of poetry and paper; her poem "Eating the Book" can be viewed at the Minnesota Center for Book Arts at the Open Book in Minneapolis; her poem "The Heart's Map" is installed at the Minnesota Children's Museum in St. Paul. Thompson received an M.F.A. in Poetry from the M.F.A. Program for Writers at Warren Wilson College in 2009.

Angela Narciso Torres was born in Brooklyn, New York, and grew up in Manila, Philippines. Her poems are available or forthcoming in *Baltimore Review, Cream City Review, Cimarron Review, Crab Orchard Review, North*

American Review, Rattle, and other publications. A graduate of the M.F.A. Program for Writers at Warren Wilson College and an associate editor at *RHINO,* she lives in Chicago.

Rosalynde Vas Dias lives in Providence, Rhode Island. She was selected as the winner of the 2012 Robert Dana Award offered by Anhinga Press and her first book, *Only Blue Body,* will be available in the fall of 2012. She earned an M.F.A. in Poetry from the M.F.A. Program for Writers at Warren Wilson College. Her poems have appeared in *The Cincinnati Review, Crazyhorse, New Orleans Review, The Pinch,* and *Matter.*

W. Vandoren Wheeler was born in Las Cruces, New Mexico. He cracked his head open on the playground in the 2nd, 4th, and 6th grades; he began writing seriously in the 8th grade. He has published poems in a dozen or so journals, including *H-NGM-N, Forklift, Ohio,* and *Swink.* He currently lives and teaches in Portland, Oregon, and is tweaking his manuscript *Lonely & Co.*

Arisa White is an M.F.A. graduate from the University of Massachusetts, Amherst, and author of the poetry chapbooks *Disposition for Shininess* and *Post Pardon;* the *San Francisco Bay Guardian* selected her for the 2010 Hot Pink List. Nominated for a Pushcart Prize in 2005, her poetry has been published widely and is featured on the recording *WORD* with the Jessica Jones Quartet. A blog editor for HER KIND, and the editorial assistant at *Dance Studio Life* magazine, Arisa is a native New Yorker, living in Oakland, California, with her partner. In 2012, virtual artists collective published her debut poetry collection, *Hurrah's Nest.*

Ross White's poems have appeared in *The Southern Review, New England Review, Poetry Daily,* and others. He won the 2012 James Larkin Pearson prize from the Poetry Society of North Carolina. A graduate of the M.F.A. Program for Writers at Warren Wilson College, he teaches Creative Writing at the University of North Carolina at Chapel Hill.

A poet, writer, and photographer, **Laurie Saurborn Young** holds an M.F.A. in Poetry from the M.F.A. Program for Writers at Warren Wilson College. *Carnavoria*, a book of poems, is forthcoming from H_NGM_N BKS. Poems have appeared in *Bat City Review, Borderlands, Crazyhorse, Mississippi Review, Narrative Magazine, New South* and elsewhere. Her photographs have been exhibited in Southampton, New York, and in Austin, Texas, where she currently lives.

Thanks

The editors would like to express our deepest gratitude to Megan Levad, francine j. harris, and Reese Okyong Kwon, each of whom stepped in and coordinated The Grind Daily Writing Series at some point. We would also like to thank Brittany Cavallaro, Marielle Prince, and Maria Carlos at Bull City Press; Alana Dunn; Wade Minter; Vievee Francis and Heidi White; the Bread Loaf Writers' Conference; and the amazing designers at Lime Tiger.